Great Moments in
Olympic
SWIMMING
& DIVING
By Karen Rosen

SportsZone
An Imprint of Abdo Publishing
www.abdopublishing.com

www.abdopublishing.com

Published by Abdo Publishing, a division of ABDO, PO Box 398166, Minneapolis, Minnesota 55439. Copyright © 2015 by Abdo Consulting Group, Inc. International copyrights reserved in all countries. No part of this book may be reproduced in any form without written permission from the publisher. SportsZone™ is a trademark and logo of Abdo Publishing.

Printed in the United States of America, North Mankato, Minnesota
042014
092014

Cover Photo: Mark J. Terrill/AP Images
Interior Photos: Mark J. Terrill/AP Images, 1, 57; Bettmann/Corbis, 6–7, 12–13; AP Images, 11, 23, 24–25, 26, 31, 32–33, 35, 39; Herbert Ludford/Bettmann/Corbis, 17; Ed Kellinovsky/AP Images, 18–19; Katsumi Kasahara/AP Images, 40–41; Ed Reinke/AP Images, 45; John Froschauer/AP Images, 46–47; Eric Draper/AP Images, 50; David J. Phillip/AP Images, 52–53; Xinhua/IMAGO/Icon SMI, 54; Franck Faugere/DPPI-SIPA/Icon SMI, 59

Editor: Chrös McDougall
Series Designer: Craig Hinton

Library of Congress Control Number: 2014932867

Cataloging-in-Publication Data
Rosen, Karen.
 Great moments in Olympic swimming & diving / Karen Rosen.
  p. cm. -- (Great moments in Olympic sports)
Includes bibliographical references and index.
ISBN 978-1-62403-399-5
1. Swimming--Juvenile literature.   2. Diving--Juvenile literature.   3. Olympics--Juvenile literature. I. Title.
797.2--dc23

2014932867

Contents

Introduction

The first Olympic swimming events were held in a bay off the Greek coast in 1896. The water was very cold and the waves were 12 feet (3.66 m) tall. "My will to live completely overcame my desire to win," said Alfred Hajos of Hungary after swimming the 1,200 meters. His time was 18 minutes, 22.2 seconds.

The 1900 Olympic events were held in the dirty River Seine in Paris, France. A lake was used in the 1904 Games in St. Louis, Missouri. By the 1908 Olympics, there was a proper pool in London, England. Because swimming was once considered unladylike, women did not compete in the Olympics until 1912 in Stockholm, Sweden.

Freestyle was the first stroke in the Olympics. Backstroke was added in 1900, breaststroke in 1908, and butterfly in 1956. In 2008, swimming returned to open water with a 10-kilometer event. Men and women each swim 17 events. There is one difference. Women swim the 800-meter freestyle while men swim 1,500 meters.

The first Olympic diving event was held at the 1904 Games. It was called "fancy diving." The Americans and Germans fought over the rules. Olympic diving for women started in 1912.

Divers compete on a 3-meter springboard and a 10-meter platform. Synchronized diving events began in 2000. Two teammates do the same dive at the same time. Men and women compete in individual and synchronized events at both heights. Divers are judged on their difficulty and execution.

1

Paris 1924
TARZAN OF THE POOL

The film producer who signed Johnny Weissmuller to play Tarzan had no idea he could swim. But Weissmuller was the king of the pool before he became a movie star as "lord of the jungle." Weissmuller grew up in Chicago, Illinois. He was 20 years old when he competed in his first Olympic Games in 1924 in Paris, France. In those days, his biggest worry was two sets of swimming brothers, not the lions and crocodiles he would later battle as Tarzan.

Johnny Weissmuller was an Olympic gold medalist in swimming before starring as Tarzan in movies.

In the 400-meter freestyle, Weissmuller dueled world-record holder Arne Borg of Sweden. Borg's brother, Ake Borg, was also in the race. The lead went back and forth between Weissmuller and Arne. Weissmuller then pulled away about 20 meters from the finish. He set a new Olympic record of 5 minutes, 4.2 seconds. Arne was second and Ake was fourth.

Two days later, Weissmuller raced the 100-meter freestyle. This time he had the Kahanamoku brothers from Hawaii on either side of him. Weissmuller was the world-record holder. He was also the first man to swim the 100 in under a minute. But Duke Kahanamoku was the defending Olympic champion. He was almost 34 years old. This was his third Olympics. Sam Kahanamoku was 21. But unlike the Borg brothers, the Kahanamoku brothers were Weissmuller's fellow Americans.

A Worthwhile Trip

Sarah "Fanny" Durack was Australia's only Olympic champion in 1912. She was also the first woman to win an Olympic swimming event. But she was almost left off the Australian team. The men in charge considered it a waste of money to send women to Stockholm, Sweden, for one swimming event. They finally said Durack and another swimmer, Mina Wylie, could go. However, the women had to raise the money for their trip. At the Games, Durack broke the world record in her 100-meter freestyle heat. She cruised to the gold, Wylie the silver. No one would call their trip a waste of money after that.

"The most important thing in this race is to get the American flag up there three times," Duke said before the race. "Let's do it."

Weissmuller won with a time of 59.0 seconds. It was a new Olympic record. Duke, who was also a legendary surfer, placed second. Sam was third. Arne Borg was fourth. The American flag went up three times.

Also that day, Weissmuller swam the anchor leg in the 4x200-meter relay. Team USA won the gold medal there, too. He also won a bronze medal in water polo. And Weissmuller could dive, too. He performed in a comedy diving act between races with a partner named Stubby.

Weissmuller went on to go undefeated at the Olympics. He again won the 100-meter freestyle in the 1928 Olympics in Amsterdam, Netherlands. He then won his fifth gold medal on the 4x200 relay.

A Swimming Legend

Weissmuller was considered part of the "Golden Age of Sports" in the 1920s. Other famous athletes included boxer Jack Dempsey, baseball player Babe Ruth, and golfer Bobby Jones. Weissmuller won 52 US titles and set 51 official world records from 100 yards to half a mile. He set other world records but did not bother to fill out the paperwork.

Weissmuller never lost a race in 10 years of amateur swimming in freestyle distances from 50 yards to half a mile. He also never lost a backstroke race. He held world records in that stroke, too. "I got bored," he said, "so I swam on my back where I could spend more time looking around."

Weissmuller was training for the 1932 Olympics to be held in Los Angeles, California. However, he stopped training to take a job advertising swimsuits. Weissmuller then was asked to try out for the part of Tarzan and got it. There was one problem. The producer said his name was too long.

"The director butted in," Weissmuller later recalled. "'Don't you ever read the papers?' he asked the producer. 'This guy is the world's greatest swimmer.'"

Weissmuller added, "Without swimming, I'd be a nobody."

Georgia Coleman

Georgia Coleman was a natural. She had been diving just six months when she made the 1928 Olympic team. She was 16. Coleman won the silver medal on platform and the bronze on springboard in Amsterdam, Netherlands. Her coach said, "At last I've found a girl who will be able to do the same difficult dives the men do." Coleman became the first woman to perform a 2½-forward somersault in competition. At the 1932 Olympics in Los Angeles, California, she won the gold in springboard. She also won the silver on platform. Tragedy struck a few years later. Coleman developed polio, pneumonia, and a liver ailment. She died in 1940 at the age of 28.

US swimmers Johnny Weissmuller, *left*, and Duke Kahanamoku hang out together at the 1924 Olympic Games in Paris, France.

He starred in 12 films as Tarzan and also had time to appear in the Billy Rose World's Fair Aquacade in 1939. Other Olympic swimmers, such as Buster Crabbe and Murray Rose, also became actors. Naturally, there were plenty of swimming scenes in Weissmuller's movies. He also said his water polo experience helped him when he was around Tarzan's chimpanzee, Cheetah.

"That's where I learned to duck," Weissmuller said. "It came in handy when Cheetah started throwing coconuts."

2

Melbourne 1956
THE DOUBLE-DOUBLE

P at McCormick performed the first double-double in Olympic diving history. It's the hardest accomplishment in diving. And it has nothing to do with double somersaults or double twisters. McCormick was the first athlete to win both the springboard and platform titles in two straight Olympic Games. McCormick did it in 1952 in Helsinki, Finland, and in 1956 in Melbourne, Australia. Only one other athlete has been able to duplicate the feat through 2012. That was American Greg Louganis in 1984 and 1988.

US diver Pat McCormick performs a dive off the 10-meter platform during the 1952 Olympic Games in Helsinki, Finland.

There's also the McCormick double. McCormick and her daughter Kelly are the only American mother-daughter duo to win Olympic medals in diving. Kelly won the silver medal in 1984 and the bronze in 1988, both in springboard diving.

A Daredevil and a Dreamer

Pat McCormick grew up in California. As a girl, she would do cannonballs off a bridge. "We loved to jump just before the boat passed under the bridge and we'd just splash them," she said. Her antics earned her the nickname "Patsy Pest."

McCormick thought swimming was boring. But she liked bouncing on the diving board. She was invited to try out for a team. At first she was scared of the 10-meter platform. It's as high as a three-story building.

Sammy Lee

US diver Sammy Lee retired from the sport to go to medical school. But he missed the sport and came back. As a 28-year-old doctor, Lee competed at the 1948 Olympic Games in London, England. He won the gold medal on platform. He also won the bronze on springboard. Lee was of Korean descent. He was the first Asian-American to win an Olympic medal. In 1952, Lee defended his platform gold medal in Helsinki, Finland. It was his thirty-second birthday. Lee was the oldest Olympic champion in diving. He later coached gold medalists Bob Webster and Greg Louganis. He also became a practicing doctor and specialized in ear diseases, including swimmer's ear.

Her experience on the platform started poorly. McCormick split her suit open. She was bruised from hitting the water.

"But when you're with your fellow divers, I don't know if that gives you the strength to not chicken out," she said.

In 1948, McCormick missed the Olympic team by .01 point. She was very upset. Then she was determined to win two gold medals at the 1952 Olympics. But McCormick didn't tell anybody. She said it was "ridiculous at that time for a woman to have a dream like that."

She did 100 dives a day, six days a week. A few weeks before the 1952 US Olympic Trials, McCormick performed in an exhibition. The pool was only 9 feet deep (2.74 m). She was used to pools being 17 feet (5.18 m) deep. McCormick crashed into the bottom. The doctor told her she would not be able to compete in the Olympic Games. But then the doctor added, "I've never seen such a hard head."

McCormick made the US Olympic team. In Helsinki, she won her first gold medal on the 3-meter springboard. She described it as "like your first kiss." She then won the platform. The Olympics did not get as much attention back then as they do today. When McCormick got back to California, some of her neighbors asked if she'd been away on vacation.

Eight months before the 1956 Olympics, McCormick had a baby boy. "All my competitors said, 'Oh, goodie, she'll never make it,'" McCormick recalled. "Well, guess what? I made it again."

In Australia, the seasons are opposite of those in the northern hemisphere. That meant the summer Olympics were in November and December instead of July or August. The schedule gave McCormick more time to prepare. And the extra time paid off. In the springboard, she won by more than 16 points. "It was one of those meets that we dream about," McCormick said. But in the platform, she missed a dive and was in fourth place after the first day.

The finals came down to her last dive, a forward 2½. That means she began facing forward and did two and a half somersaults.

Marjorie Gestring

American Marjorie Gestring won the gold medal in springboard diving at the 1936 Olympics in Berlin, Germany. She was 13 years, 267 days old. She is the youngest person to win an individual Olympic gold medal in any sport. The youngest gold medalist in a team sport might have been a French boy at the 1900 Olympics in Paris, France. From a photo, he looks younger than 10 years old. The Dutch rowing team asked him to be its coxswain in coxed pairs. Researchers have never found out his name. Today's divers must be at least 14 years old to compete in the Olympics.

"They blew the whistle; I hit that tower so hard, you could see it just shake," she said. "I spun it, I dropped it, and it looked like a cup full of bubbles. I sort of cry sometimes when I think of that. When I popped up I heard [scores of] 10, 9½, and 10."

McCormick finished with 84.85 points and led a US sweep. Juno Irwin, a mother of three, was second with 81.64. Paula Jean Myers was third with 81.58. McCormick later founded the Pat McCormick Educational Foundation. Her program called "Pat's Champs" encouraged children to stay in school and chase their dreams.

Tokyo 1964
A WILD RIDE

Dawn Fraser broke a lot of records. She also broke a lot of rules. The Australian swimmer won four Olympic gold medals and four silver medals. She was the first swimmer to win the same Olympic event three times—the 100-meter freestyle in 1956, 1960, and 1964. Plus she set 27 individual world records and was part of 12 team world records. Fraser held the world record in the 100 freestyle for more than 15 years.

Fraser was the youngest of eight children. She had asthma and began swimming to help strengthen her

Australian swimmer Dawn Fraser was known for swimming really fast and getting into trouble.

19

lungs. It turned out she was pretty good at it. In early 1956, Fraser broke the 100-meter freestyle world record that had stood 20 years. But by the time the Olympic Games began in Melbourne, Australia, fellow Australian Lorraine Crapp held the record of 1 minute, 2.4 seconds.

In her autobiography, *Below the Surface*, Fraser said she had a nightmare before the final. In her dream, she had honey on her feet and the water was spaghetti. "I fought with it and kept going up and down in the one place, like a yo-yo," she wrote.

In the actual race, Fraser could move freely. She beat Crapp with a world-record time of 1:02.0. However, Crapp got revenge in the 400-meter freestyle. She won the gold and Fraser the silver. They then teamed up for gold on the 4x100-meter freestyle relay.

Felipe Munoz

Felipe Munoz was nicknamed Tibio. That's Spanish for "lukewarm." His father came from the village of Aguascalientes (meaning "hot water"). His mother was from Rio Frio ("cold river"). But Munoz heated up the pool at the 1968 Olympics in Mexico City, Mexico. The host country had not won a gold medal after 10 days of competition. Hundreds of thousands of Mexican people watched the 200-meter breaststroke on TV. Munoz was in fourth place at the halfway point. With 50 meters left, he was picking up steam. Finally, Munoz passed world-record holder Vladimir Kosinsky of the Soviet Union. All of Mexico celebrated his sizzling victory.

Fraser did not lose any 100-meter races between the 1956 and 1960 Olympics. She won in Rome, Italy, in 1960 with an Olympic record. But then Fraser got in big trouble. At a team meeting the next day, she got in an argument.

At lunch that day, she had eaten a big meal. Then a team manager told her to go the pool. He wanted her to swim the butterfly leg in a heat of the medley relay. Fraser wouldn't go. She said she was full. Her teammates were so mad they would not speak to her the rest of the trip.

But they did swim with her. Fraser won silver medals in the 4x100 freestyle relay and in a new event for women, the 4x100 medley relay. However, she had broken several rules while in Rome, including not wearing the national sweat suit to receive her gold medal. She also was accused of taking part in an unauthorized race in Switzerland. As a result, Fraser was banned from international competitions for two years.

On the Comeback

In 1962, Fraser became the first woman to swim the 100-meter freestyle in under one minute. She lowered the record to 58.9 seconds in February 1964. The next month, Fraser was in a horrible car accident. Her mother was killed and Fraser was injured. She had to wear a brace on her neck and back. Her swimming career was threatened.

Fraser still attempted to come back for the 1964 Games in Tokyo, Japan. And she indeed swam in her third Olympics at age 27. Her teammates called her "Granny." But Fraser was still a rebel. Australian officials told her not to go to the Opening Ceremony. They wanted her to rest. She went anyway.

It didn't seem to hurt her. Fraser held off American Sharon Stouder in the final with an Olympic record of 59.5 seconds. Stouder, who swam 59.9, was the second woman to break one minute.

Fraser saw the Australian flag raised in her honor for the third time. But she wanted another flag. Late one night, Fraser led a raid to steal a souvenir flag from the Emperor's Palace. She was arrested. The charges were dropped. The Emperor wasn't upset. In fact, he gave her the flag.

Misty Hyman Scores an Upset

American Misty Hyman was known for her underwater sideways "fish kick." Then a rule change took away her advantage. Hyman had doubts she could remain a world-class swimmer. Asthma and sinus trouble caused more problems. She almost quit. Meanwhile, Australian Susie O'Neill was having a great year. She broke the 19-year-old world record in the 200-meter butterfly. O'Neil was a huge favorite at the 2000 Olympics in Sydney, Australia. But Hyman swam to victory. When she looked at the scoreboard, she couldn't believe she'd won. Now Hyman is famous for her stunning Olympic upset.

Australia's Dawn Fraser, *center*, shows off her gold medal in the 100-meter freestyle at the 1964 Olympics. Americans Sharon Stouder, *left*, and Kathleen Ellis, *right*, won the silver and bronze medals, respectively.

Later, Fraser's teammates selected her to carry the Australian flag in the Closing Ceremony. But Australian officials were furious about Fraser's antics. They suspended her for 10 years.

The ban was lifted after four years, but her swimming career was over. As the International Swimming Hall of Fame noted, "Her good times are not all in the water."

Munich 1972
SPITZ FOR SEVEN

Mark Spitz left the 1968 Olympic Games extremely disappointed. He called it "the worst meet of my life." At those Games in Mexico City, Mexico, he had won two gold medals, one silver, and one bronze. For Spitz, that was underachieving.

Spitz was used to success at an early age. He was the world's best swimmer in the 10-and-under age group. In 1967, he won five gold medals at the Pan American Games. That is an Olympic-like competition involving athletes from North and South America.

US swimmer Mark Spitz went into the 1972 Olympic Games in Munich, West Germany, hoping to win a record seven gold medals.

Mark Spitz surges away from Great Britain's Brian Brinkley during a 200-meter butterfly heat at the 1972 Olympics.

The performance made Spitz believe he could win six events at the 1968 Olympics.

In Mexico City, Spitz finished second in his best event, the 100-meter butterfly. He settled for the bronze in the 100 freestyle. His only gold medals were on the two US freestyle relays. Spitz's last event was the 200 butterfly. By that time, he had lost his confidence. He finished last of eight swimmers in the final.

The performance did not discourage him. By 1972, Spitz had an even more ambitious goal. He wanted to win seven gold medals at the Games in Munich, West Germany. American Don Schollander had won four in 1964. That was the record for a swimmer.

"If I know I'm the best and feel it, and people then think I'm cocky, there's nothing I can do about it," said Spitz, then 22, before the Olympics.

This time the 200 butterfly was Spitz's first event. He won in world-record time. The same night, Spitz swam a leg on the 4x100-meter freestyle relay. Another gold, another world record. His next victory came in the 200-meter freestyle. Spitz then won the 100 butterfly. He swam a leg on the winning 4x200 freestyle relay, too. That gave him five gold

Anthony Nesty

In 1988, Suriname had just one Olympic-size swimming pool. The small South American country had never won an Olympic medal. Then Anthony Nesty upset Matt Biondi in the 100-meter butterfly. Nesty touched the wall .01 before the American favorite. "What if I had grown my fingernails longer?" Biondi wondered. Nesty, who trained in Florida, was the first black swimmer to win an Olympic gold medal. "I think when I won they were scrambling because they didn't expect to play the national anthem for Suriname," Nesty said. Meanwhile, Biondi went on to win five gold medals at those Games in Seoul, South Korea.

medals. Spitz had equaled the record set by Italian fencer Nedo Nadi in 1920 and Finnish runner Paavo Nurmi in 1924.

"You could say I am very thrilled at what I accomplished," he said.

But Spitz wasn't looking forward to his next race. He wanted to skip the 100-meter freestyle. During the 4x100 freestyle relay, US teammate Jerry Heidenreich had swum faster than Spitz.

"I'd rather win six out of six, or even four out of four, than six out of seven," Spitz said. "It's reached a point where my self-esteem comes into it. I just don't want to lose."

Spitz told his old coach, Sherm Chavoor, that he was tired. Spitz thought he should rest for the 4x100 medley relay. "Six gold medals isn't so bad," Spitz said he told the coach.

"You mean five gold medals," Chavoor replied.

"What do you mean?" said Spitz.

"Listen, Mark, if you don't swim the 100 meters, you're out of the relay. You might as well go home now," Chavoor said. "They'll say you're 'chicken'—that you're afraid to face Jerry Heidenreich."

Spitz got the message. He finished second in both of his heats. But in the final, Spitz beat Heidenreich. He set his sixth world record. He now had the record for most gold medals.

The next day, Spitz swam the butterfly leg on the winning 4x100 medley relay. Heidenreich swam the freestyle leg. It was the seventh world record for Spitz. He now had seven gold medals and seven world records.

No Celebration

The next day, Spitz went to the media center for a news conference. But something terrible had happened earlier that morning. Palestinian terrorists broke into the Olympic Village. Within 24 hours, 11 Israeli coaches and athletes would be dead.

Spitz, who was Jewish like the murdered Israelis, was given six armed guards. He was put on the first flight to London, England. While he

The Thorpedo

Ian Thorpe was a world champion by age 15. "The Thorpedo" had size 17 feet, which helped him kick. He was the hometown hero at the 2000 Olympics in Sydney, Australia, winning three gold medals. But Thorpe couldn't win everything. The Australian lost the 200-meter freestyle and his world record to Pieter van den Hoogenband of the Netherlands. Going into the 2004 Olympics, Thorpe again held the world record. The final featured the four fastest men in history. They were Thorpe, van den Hoogenband, American Michael Phelps, and Australian Grant Hackett. The Dutchman led almost the whole race. This time, though, Thorpe surged past him to win. Phelps was third.

was there, he posed for a famous photo. Spitz wore only his red, white, and blue swimsuit and seven gold medals. More than 1 million posters were sold.

Still affected by the tragedy that struck his fellow Olympians, Spitz later said of the photo shoot, "I was hardly in the mood to do that poster, but we went to a studio and shot it anyway."

He liked another photo better. It showed his teammates carrying him around the pool after the last relay. "Having a tribute from your teammates," he said, "is a feeling that can never be duplicated."

Montreal 1976
IN THE FACE
OF DOPING

The East German women's swimming team had one of the greatest turnarounds in history. The squad did not win any gold medals at the 1972 Olympic Games in Munich, West Germany. Four years later, the East Germans won 11 of the 13 events at the 1976 Games in Montreal, Canada. The team's biggest star, Kornelia Ender, became the first woman to win four swimming gold medals in one Olympics. But some swimmers were suspicious. They thought the East Germans were doping, or using performance-enhancing drugs (PEDs).

Kornelia Ender of East Germany, *left*, dominated the swimming events at the 1976 Olympics, but some suspected her of doping.

Shirley Babashoff was the best freestyle swimmer in the United States. At the 1976 Olympic Trials, Babashoff won all of the freestyle events. She had the speed to win the 100 and 200. Babashoff also had the endurance for the 400 and 800. She set three American records in the preliminaries. In the finals, Babashoff set three more American records and the world record in the 800. But in Montreal, she won four silver medals. She lost every time to East German swimmers.

Babashoff made comments implying that the East Germans were doping. She noticed how big the East Germans were. Their voices were deep. These are sometimes effects of PEDs. But Babashoff was called a poor sport. The media nicknamed her "Surly Shirley." An East German official said, "We came here to swim, not to sing."

Mixed Results

Swimming races today are timed with very precise automatic devices. In 1960, races were decided by eyeballs. John Devitt of Australia and Lance Larson of the United States finished in a dead heat in the 100-meter freestyle in Rome, Italy. Two of the three first-place judges thought Devitt won. Two of the second-place judges were certain he was second. The timekeepers gave Larson 55.0, 55.1, and 55.1 seconds. Each timed Devitt at 55.2. An unofficial electronic timer also picked Larson. The Swedish chief judge was not supposed to make the decision. He did, though, giving Devitt the win. Larson's time was changed to 55.2. The US protested for four years to no avail.

East German swimmer Ulrike Richter celebrates after winning a gold medal in the 100-meter backstroke at the 1976 Olympic Games in Montreal, Canada.

The first event in Montreal was the 4x100-meter medley relay. The East German team set a world record of 4 minutes, 7.95 seconds. Team USA, anchored by Babashoff, was second in 4:14.55.

Babashoff took fifth in the 100. Two East Germans finished ahead of her. She finished second to Ender in the 200. She then took second in the 400 and 800 behind Petra Thumer. The 15-year-old East German set world records in both races.

The final women's swimming event was the 4x100 freestyle relay. The United States had beaten East Germany in this event in 1972. Could they do it again? Ender, the 100-meter freestyle gold medalist, swam first. She gave East Germany a 1.16-second lead over American Kim Peyton. Petra Priemer, the 100-meter silver medalist, went second for East Germany. But Wendy Boglioli helped Team USA close the gap.

On the next leg, American Jill Sterkel passed Andrea Pollack. Sterkel's time was 55.78 seconds. That gave the US a .40-second lead. Now it was Babashoff's turn. She kept the lead. Her time was 56.28 seconds. The United States finished in 3:44.82. It was a new world record. The Americans broke the previous record held by East Germany by almost four seconds. East Germany was second in 3:45.50.

It was the only US gold medal in women's swimming at the 1976 Olympics. The only other event East Germany did not win was the 200-meter breaststroke. Marina Koshevaia led a 1-2-3 sweep for the Soviet Union. East Germany was fourth, fifth, and sixth.

Four years later, the United States boycotted the 1980 Olympics in Moscow, Soviet Union. East Germany again dominated with 11 gold medals. The tables turned in 1984. East Germany boycotted while the United States won 11 gold medals.

Both countries competed in 1988. East Germany won 10 events, with Kristin Otto winning a record six golds. Janet Evans won all three US gold medals. She won the 400 free, 800 free, and 400 individual medley.

Doping Revealed

In 1989, East Germany and West Germany reunited to create an independent Germany. In 1990, Ender revealed that she was given frequent injections while she was a swimmer. She did not know what kind of drugs were in them. Finally, in 2007, East German officials admitted

Turning the Page

World War II ended in 1945. But it was still in people's thoughts in 1956. Two 17-year-old swimmers, Murray Rose of Australia and Tsuyoshi Yamanaka of Japan, came from countries on opposing sides in the war. They met at the 1956 Olympics in Melbourne, Australia. Rose defeated Yamanaka at 400 meters. He then took a big lead in the 1,500. Yamanaka closed the gap, but Rose held him off to win. "I knew the crowd was watching us closely," Rose said. Both swimmers smiled, then embraced. "Behind us we heard the crowd cheering," Rose said. He recalled that a newspaper photo caption the next day declared, "The war is finally over."

The US 4x100-meter freestyle relay team celebrates as Shirley Babashoff swims the final leg en route to the gold medal at the 1976 Olympics in Montreal, Canada.

that thousands of athletes had been doped without their knowledge. The reason was to promote the country through success in sports.

Babashoff's coach, Mark Schubert, said of his swimmer, "She was the only one that had the guts to speak out back then. If anybody had the right to speak out, it was her because she was the one that was cheated out of Olympic gold medals."

Efforts to convince the International Olympic Committee (IOC) to take away the East German medals have failed. That would give Babashoff five gold medals and one bronze medal from 1976. Had she won five gold medals in Montreal, Babashoff would have been one of the most decorated swimmers in history. No action has ever been taken.

Better than Chocolate

One 1936 Olympian was motivated by chocolate. Before the 400-meter freestyle, Ragnhild Hveger got a box of chocolates as a gift. The 15-year-old Danish swimmer shared with everyone except Hendrika "Rie" Mastenbroek. That made the 17-year-old Dutch swimmer mad. Mastenbroek passed Hveger in the final 25 meters of the race. She thought, "This is much better than a piece of chocolate." Mastenbroek was the first woman to win four medals at one Olympics. She was very generous. She donated one of her three gold medals to charity. It was used to raise money to build a village for disabled people.

6

Seoul 1988
BOUNCING BACK

G reg Louganis performed amazing dives throughout his career. The American won four Olympic gold medals and one silver medal from 1976 to 1988. But there's one dive people remember most—one they still can't believe. That's the dive on which Louganis hit his head on the springboard.

It was the way he bounced back that defined him as a champion.

Louganis was adopted as a baby and had a difficult childhood. He stuttered when he talked. Kids teased him

US diver Greg Louganis bangs his head on the springboard during a preliminary-round dive at the 1988 Olympic Games in Seoul, South Korea.

and beat him up. He started to smoke and drink when he was very young. Louganis also suffered from depression. Diving gave him a reason to feel good about himself.

Dr. Sammy Lee, the Olympic champion, started coaching Louganis in 1975. "The first time I saw him I knew he would be the greatest diver in history if he got the right coach," Lee said.

Louganis moved in with Lee and qualified for the 1976 Olympics in Montreal, Canada. He won the silver medal on platform behind Italian Klaus Dibiasi. On the awards platform, Dibiasi leaned down and whispered: "In four years, you'll be up here."

The United States boycotted the 1980 Olympics in Moscow, Soviet Union. That meant Louganis had to wait eight years for his next

A Greek Triumph

As the host country, Greece was given the opportunity to enter a team that had not qualified in the 2004 synchronized springboard diving event. Nikolaos Siranidis and Thomas Bimis were a respectable fourth place with one dive to go. China led by 12 points. But China's Wang Kenan lost control of his last dive, scoring zero points. China fell into last place. Dmitri Sautin of the world champion Russian team then hit his head on the board. Russia dropped to seventh. The Americans had a bad takeoff. That left the Greeks. Their spectacular inward 3½ somersault tuck dive gave Greece its first gold medal of the Games.

Olympics. He hardly sat still though. The Californian won 19 consecutive international competitions from 1982 to 1987. At the 1982 World Championships, Louganis was the first diver to score perfect 10s on a dive from all seven judges. Louganis won the springboard and platform events at the 1984 Olympics in Los Angeles, California, by large margins. A British newspaper called him "Mr. Perfect."

But in 1988, Louganis lost twice to Tan Liangde of China. He knew he would have to be at the top of his game to win at the Games in Seoul, South Korea.

Head Games

In Seoul, Louganis was leading the springboard preliminaries after eight dives. His ninth was a reverse 2½ somersault in the pike position. But when he left the board, he jumped directly up instead of pushing away from the board. Louganis flew high into the air and began flipping. But on his way down, he cracked his head on the edge of the board. The crowd gasped.

"I jumped off the board and heard this big clank," he said that day. "That's my perception of the dive—I think my pride was hurt more than anything."

Louganis landed in the water without his usual grace. Years later, he recalled, "I went crashing into the water and I thought, 'What was that? Was that my head?'" The diver was bleeding when he came out of the water. A doctor quickly stitched him up. Louganis had only 30 minutes to perform his next dive.

"I had absolutely no confidence in myself," Louganis remembered. "I didn't know what I did wrong, so I didn't know how to fix it."

His coach, Ron O'Brien, gave him a pep talk. "I finally turned to Ron and said, 'We've worked too long and hard to give up now,'" Louganis recalled.

The crowd was surprised to see him on the board. Louganis thumped his hand over his chest as if his heart was pumping like mad. The crowd

Micki King

American Micki King was poised to win the springboard diving gold medal at the 1968 Olympics in Mexico City, Mexico. She was leading after eight dives. But King smacked the board on her ninth. She broke her left forearm. Despite the injury, King performed one more dive. She finished fourth, just short of a medal. King spent months in a cast and a year in recovery. At the 1972 Olympics, King was again in first after eight dives. Just like in Mexico City, her tenth and final dive was a reverse 1½ somersault with 1½ twists. She hit the dive to win by almost 16 points.

Greg Louganis performs a dive off the 10-meter platform at the 1988 Olympic Games.

laughed. Louganis felt like they were in this together. "I was like, 'I have no idea what's going to happen, but let's just go for it," he said.

He scored 87.12 points on his 1½ somersault with 3½ twists. It was the highest score of the day. The crowd gave him a standing ovation.

Louganis hit all of his dives in the final. That included the one on which he hit his head. He easily won the gold medal. A week later, Louganis won another gold on the platform. He was the first male diver to achieve the "double-double." The only other diver to accomplish the feat was Pat McCormick. She did it in 1952 and 1956.

7

Sydney 2000
A SURPRISE SPLASH

Laura Wilkinson was a gymnast until she grew too tall for the sport. At age 15, she decided to try diving, which also was composed of flips and twists. A teacher told Wilkinson she was too old to start a new sport. In this case, Wilkinson didn't listen to her teacher. She took the plunge off the 10-meter platform.

Nine months later, Wilkinson was kicked off her high school diving team. She says somebody on the team called her a "waste of space." That made Wilkinson even more determined. She continued diving and got better

Laura Wilkinson performs a back 2½ dive off the 10-meter platform at the 2000 US Olympic Trials.

in a hurry. The next year, in 1995, Wilkinson became US champion for the first time. She also won a bronze medal at the World Cup. The World Cup is one of the sport's biggest international events.

Wilkinson earned a scholarship to attend college at the University of Texas. However, she took time off to train for the 2000 Olympic Games in Sydney, Australia. Then disaster struck. In March, three and a half months before the 2000 US Olympic Trials, Wilkinson had an accident while training on dry land. She broke her right foot in three places. A bone was sticking into the sole of her foot.

Against All Odds

Wilkinson had a cast on her foot for 10 weeks. She still went to the Trials and made the US Olympic team. But the diving world had changed since the United States dominated in the early Olympics. China had won every Olympic women's platform title since 1984. And two Chinese divers looked like they would continue the streak in Sydney. They were first and second going into the final. Wilkinson was in eighth place.

The 22-year-old Wilkinson seemed very far away from a medal. And she was wearing a protective shoe on her foot whenever she walked on the pool deck or up the stairs to the platform. Could someone really win a gold medal with a broken foot?

After two dives, Li Na of China ranked first. Anne Montminy of Canada was second, followed by Sang Xue of China. Wilkinson was fifth. Then Li and Sang made mistakes on their third dives. Montminy and her Canadian teammate, Emilie Heymans, also lost points on this round. Wilkinson, meanwhile, performed her reverse 2½ somersault and was nearly perfect. She was suddenly in first place.

Wilkinson's next-to-last dive was an inward 2½ somersault pike. She was nervous about her takeoff, afraid she would hit the platform. Wilkinson had blown the same dive in the preliminaries and the semifinals. Her coach, Ken Armstrong, pulled Wilkinson aside. He whispered in her ear, "Do this for Hilary."

Chinese Stars

China has been the top country in women's diving since the 1980s. Gao Min was Olympic springboard champion in 1988 and 1992. Fu Mingxia won the platform in 1992 and then won both events in 1996. She then retired. When Fu came back two years later, she had a rival. Guo Jingjing beat Fu five times before the 2000 Olympics. They were also partners in synchronized springboard diving. In Sydney, they won the silver medal. In the individual springboard event, Guo led after two dives. But Fu dominated the final three rounds to win the gold. She then retired again. Guo was champion in 2004 and 2008 in both springboard and synchronized springboard.

Laura Wilkinson dives off the 10-meter platform during the 2000 Olympic Games in Sydney, Australia.

He was referring to her friend and teammate, Hilary Grivich, who was killed in a car accident in 1997. Grivich was a world-class gymnast who became a diver.

"It kind of took me by surprise," Wilkinson said. "But it was another motivation. It's good to fight for something."

She made the long climb up to the tower. Wilkinson did everything she was supposed to do. The judges agreed. Her scores ranged from 8.5 to 9.5.

With one dive to go, Wilkinson held a tiny lead over Montminy. She led Li by more than five points. All three hit their last dives. Wilkinson did a back 2½ somersault with a half twist. Li performed a forward 3½ somersault. Wilkinson beat Li by 1.74 points. It was the smallest margin of victory in the event since the 1964 Games. Because Montminy's dive was not as hard as the others, she dropped to third.

"We had a lot of trials and tribulations to get here," Wilkinson said. "The day I broke my foot, I thought my dreams were over."

Wilkinson was the first American woman since Lesley Bush in 1964 to win the platform diving title. "This year, our goal was not just to make the Olympic team," Wilkinson said, "but to win a medal, and not just a medal, but a gold one."

David Boudia

The once-proud US diving tradition had hit a rough patch. At the 2004 and 2008 Olympics, the United States did not win any medals. The dry spell ended at the 2012 Olympics in London, England. The United States won two bronze medals in synchronized diving. The final chance for an individual medal was men's platform. American David Boudia, who had won a bronze on synchronized platform, was eighteenth in the preliminaries. He moved up to third in the semifinals. The final was tight. Boudia won on his final dive by 1.8 points. He beat world champion Qiu Bo of China. Tom Daley of Great Britain, the crowd favorite, was third.

8

Beijing 2008
EIGHT FOR EIGHT

Swimmer Michael Phelps has won more Olympic medals than many countries. His 22 total medals is a record for an athlete in any sport. Phelps has also earned a record 18 gold medals. He won some of his races easily. He won one by a fingernail. And he won eight of those gold medals at the 2008 Olympic Games in Beijing, China. That amazing run broke the record of seven Olympic gold medals set by fellow swimmer Mark Spitz in 1972.

Team USA's Michael Phelps dives into the pool to start the 100-meter butterfly at the 2008 Olympic Games in Beijing, China.

Michael Phelps, *right*, and Garrett Weber-Gale celebrate after teammate Jason Lezak completed a comeback victory in the 4x100-meter freestyle relay at the 2008 Olympics.

Phelps was competing in his third Olympics in Beijing. The "Baltimore Bullet" was only 15 at his first Games in 2000 in Sydney, Australia. His best finish there was fifth place in the 200-meter butterfly. Six months later, Phelps broke the world record in that event. He was the youngest male to set a swimming world record.

At the 2004 Olympics in Athens, Greece, Phelps won six gold medals and two bronze medals. It was an amazing accomplishment. However, it was also slightly disappointing. Phelps had been trying to equal Spitz's record. Speedo, his swimsuit sponsor, had offered him a $1 million bonus if he could do it.

Chasing History

Beijing gave Phelps another chance to try for the record and the $1 million bonus. He had no intention of falling short. Phelps first won the 400-meter individual medley. The next day, the US team came from behind to win the 4x100-meter freestyle relay. Jason Lezak, swimming the anchor leg, chased down the French team. That kept Phelps's hopes afloat.

Phelps won the 200-meter freestyle for his third gold. In 2004, he won the bronze in this event. The next day, Phelps had two races. He first won

The Amazing Chase

Michael Phelps could not win eight gold medals alone. He needed help from his teammates on three relays at the 2008 Olympics. Without Jason Lezak, Phelps's golden streak would have ended after two events. His second final was the 4x100-meter freestyle relay. Phelps set an American record of 47.51 seconds leading off. However, Eamon Sullivan of Australia was faster. Team USA pulled ahead in the second leg. Then France took the lead. Lezak was the last US hope. He caught France's Alain Bernard and posted the fastest relay split in history, 46.06 seconds. Phelps's quest for eight Olympic gold medals lived on for another day.

the 200-meter butterfly. Less than an hour later, he swam the first leg on the winning 4x200 freestyle relay. Now Phelps had five gold medals. His sixth gold came in the 200-meter individual medley. It was also his sixth world record.

Everything was on the line in the 100-meter butterfly. Phelps could tie the record with his seventh gold medal and earn the $1 million. Not everyone was rooting for him. Milorad Cavic of Serbia said before the race, "It would be good for the sport if he lost."

Phelps said those words fired him up. However, he did not get a good start. Surprisingly, Phelps was in seventh place out of eight swimmers at the turn. Cavic was the leader. Phelps had to make up more than half a second in the final 50 meters to win. Could he do it?

When they got close to the wall, Cavic was sure he had won. He glided in. Phelps chopped his stroke, reaching for the wall. With his wingspan of 6 feet, 7 inches, he slammed into the touchpad that records the time. Phelps looked at the scoreboard. He was overjoyed to see a "1" by his name. He had won by .01 of a second.

The Serbs protested. Officials looked at the video frame by frame. They said Phelps had definitely won. Underwater images proved Phelps had won by the smallest of margins.

Milorad Cavic of Serbia, *right*, races Michael Phelps to the finish line in the 100-meter butterfly at the 2008 Olympics.

"As soon as I took the last half stroke, to be honest I thought that I had lost the race," Phelps said. "That was the difference. If I had glided, I would have lost. I guess I'm blessed."

His winning time of 50.58 seconds was an Olympic record. However, it was Phelps's only finals race in Beijing in which he did not set the world record. Spitz had won seven gold medals with seven world records. Still, Phelps swam a more challenging program than Spitz. In 1972, Spitz swam only freestyle and butterfly races that were 200 meters or shorter. Phelps swam up to 400 meters in all four strokes. He also swam in more preliminary races.

"It goes to show you that not only is this guy the greatest swimmer of all time and the greatest Olympian of all time, he's maybe the greatest athlete of all time," Spitz said. "He's the greatest racer who ever walked the planet."

Phelps still had one more race in which to set the record for gold medals. And indeed he won his eighth gold medal on the 4x100 medley relay on the last day of Olympic swimming competition. Phelps swam the butterfly leg.

Phelps's performance in Beijing made him a national star. He took some time off from swimming. Companies hired him to endorse their products. Ultimately, Phelps returned to the pool, though. And he went into the 2012 Olympics in London, England, with high hopes. He expected to retire after that. And he wanted to go out on top. Phelps's

Missy Franklin

Missy Franklin has been called the "female Michael Phelps." At the 2012 Olympics, the teenager was the first woman to compete in seven events. One night, Franklin swam a 200-meter freestyle semifinal and the 100 backstroke final within 14 minutes. "I'm only 17. There's no such thing as fatigue," she said. Franklin set a world record in the 200-meter backstroke to earn the second of her four gold medals in London, England. The smiling, fun-loving Colorado native also played a big part in the famous video made by the US swimming team. They lip-synced to the song "Call Me Maybe."

Michael Phelps celebrates after winning his eighth
gold medal in the 2008 Olympics, this one in
the 4x100-meter medley relay.

performance wasn't as dominant as it had been in Athens and Beijing. But

he added four gold and two silver medals. That gave him 22 medals. He

passed Soviet gymnast Larisa Latynina as the most decorated Olympian

of all time. She had won 18 medals from 1956 to 1964. Phelps had indeed

gone out on top.

Great Olympians

Janet Evans (USA)
The swimmer won three gold medals at the 1988 Olympics and another gold medal in 1992.

Missy Franklin (USA)
In 2012, the 17-year-old was the first woman to swim seven events at an Olympics. She won four gold medals and a bronze.

Dawn Fraser (Australia)
She was the first swimmer, male or female, to win the same event three straight times. Fraser won the 100-meter freestyle in 1956, 1960, and 1964.

Fu Mingxia (China)
She won the 1992 platform gold medal, both springboard and platform in 1996, and another springboard in 2000.

Sammy Lee (USA)
The first Asian-American to win an Olympic gold medal, Lee won the platform diving title in 1948 and repeated in 1952.

Greg Louganis (USA)
After winning a silver medal on platform in 1976, he achieved the double-double in 1984 and 1988.

Pat McCormick (USA)
She won the springboard and platform titles in 1952 and 1956 to become the first diver to achieve the double-double.

Kristin Otto (East Germany)
Otto won a women's record six gold medals at the 1988 Olympics. However, she was later revealed to have used PEDs.

Michael Phelps (USA)
He won a record 22 Olympic medals, including 18 gold, from 2004 to 2012. He also won a record eight gold medals in 2008.

Mark Spitz (USA)
Spitz posted seven world records in winning seven gold medals at the 1972 Olympics. He won four medals, two gold, in 1968.

Glossary

ANCHOR
The last of four competitors on a relay team.

BOYCOTT
Refusing participation as a form of protest.

COXSWAIN
A member of a rowing team who is in command of the boat but does not row.

DOPING
The illegal use of a drug to get an unfair advantage.

HEAT
One of multiple races in an event. In the Olympics, many races have preliminary heats to determine the fastest swimmers who make the finals.

ENDORSE
To promote a company or its products in return for compensation.

LEG
One of four positions on a swimming relay team.

MEDLEY
A swimming race that involves all four strokes: backstroke, breaststroke, butterfly, and freestyle. In a medley relay, each of the four team members swims one of the four strokes.

PIKE
A diving position in which the legs remain straight while the body bends at the waist.

SCHOLARSHIP
Financial assistance to help pay for college. Great athletes earn scholarships to represent their schools through sports.

TUCK
A diving position in which the knees are bent and pulled into the body.

For More
Information

SELECTED BIBLIOGRAPHY

Burnton, Simon. "50 Stunning Olympic Moments No. 37: Mark Spitz Wins Seven Swimming Golds." *The Guardian*. The Guardian Media Group, 8 June 2012. Web. 7 Feb. 2014.

Crouse, Karen. "Another Pool Day Belongs to Phelps and Franklin." *The New York Times*. The New York Times Co., 3 Aug. 2012. Web. 7 Feb. 2014.

Landler, Mark. "Sydney 2000: Diving; From a Broken Dream to a Gold Medal." *The New York Times*. The New York Times Co., 25 Sept. 2000. Web. 7 Feb. 2014.

Lutton, Phil. "Meet Missy, the Female Michael Phelps Who's Turning Down $2m to Go to College." *The Sydney Morning Herald*. Fairfax Media, 3 Aug. 2012. Web. 7 Feb. 2014.

Plaschke, Bill. "Greg Louganis Remembers the Olympic Dive That Made History." *Los Angeles Times*, Tribune Co., 12 Sept. 2013. Web. 7 Feb. 2014.

FURTHER READINGS

Daley, Tom. *My Story*. London: Michael Joseph, 2012.

Dzidrums, Christine. *Missy Franklin: Swimming Sensation: Y Not Girl Volume 3*. Whittier, CA: Creative Media Publishing, 2013.

Foster, Richard J. *Mark Spitz: The Extraordinary Life of an Olympic Champion*. Solana Beach, CA: Santa Monica Press, 2008.

Phelps, Michael, and Brian Cazeneuve. *Beneath the Surface: My Story*. New York: Sports Publishing, 2012.

Wallechinsky, David, and Jaime Loucky. *The Complete Book of the Olympics: 2012 Edition*. London, Aurum Press, 2012.

WEBSITES

To learn more about Great Moments in Olympic Sports, visit **booklinks.abdopublishing.com**. These links are routinely monitored and updated to provide the most current information available.

PLACES TO VISIT

International Swimming Hall of Fame
One Hall of Fame Drive
Ft. Lauderdale, FL 33316
(954) 462-6536
www.ishof.org
The museum and exhibit hall opened in 1965. It occupies an elevated wave-shaped building that sits at the entrance to the Hall of Fame Aquatic Complex. The history of swimming, diving, water polo, and synchronized swimming is traced through more than 40 exhibits. The hall of fame plans to move from Fort Lauderdale in February 2015.

US Olympic Training Center
1750 E Boulder St.
Colorado Springs, CO 80909
(719) 866-4618
www.teamusa.org
The US Olympic team has welcomed more than 1.6 million visitors to its headquarters in Colorado Springs, Colorado. In addition to extensive training facilities for elite athletes, the USOTC offers visitors the chance to discover US Olympic history through its indoor and outdoor exhibitions and installations. Walking tours are conducted daily.

Index

ABOUT THE AUTHOR

As the daughter of a track coach in Auburn, Alabama, Karen Rosen grew up holding the tape at the finish line. She attended her first Olympics in Montreal, Canada, in 1976 on a family vacation and worked for ABC at the 1984 Games in Los Angeles, California. Rosen has covered every Olympics since 1992 as a journalist, including those in Barcelona, Spain, where her father, Mel, was the US men's track coach.